21 Messages

Tiny motivations

Akarsha Alapati

BookLeaf Publishing

India | USA | UK

Made with ❤ on the BookLeaf Publishing Platform
www.bookleafpub.in
www.bookleafpub.com

Dedication

To every person who turned into Blake when they were low or excited 😊 😊

To my amma and nana, they know me like a book.

Preface

Every time I wrote is when I has a sudden high, suddenly inspired, sudden urge to say something and tell everybody and myself, this is what it is. I had to capture on the fly and tuck it away. Had to have a book. And so these really are messages, more than poems. Rhyming is what I feel sets an easy cozy bond though they are a million ways to write poems. "Dwell in possibility."- Emily Dickinson, this was the quote in my email signature for years! Act on your spark amigos.

I hope every poem sets you thinking and please do message me as a pen pal or otherwise. We can any hash out any of the subjects.

My insta handle @alapatiakarsha

Would love to hear your take. Much love. Much catharsis.

Akarsha.

#Iwritewhatyoufeel #21Messages

Acknowledgements

It would be insane to not acknowledge my father who passed on his wordsmith genes. He always bought me a fiction and a non fiction book together for every birthday, and I needed to read both! No "The Magic Faraway Tree" or "Oliver Twist" was bought without a "Divine Romance" (Paramahamsa Yogananda) or "Notes to Myself" (Hugh Prather). Love him for that.

Thank my school librarian Mrs Susan Iype for her endless suggestions and my English teachers who brought alive Shylock from "The Tempest" or the wicked witches of Grimms fairy tales not to forget dear Mr Ruskin Bond and his conquests.

A few bottled thoughts in this book now. Thank you Book Leaf for giving us this window, a great gesture to allow many artists of the written word knock themselves out. We all thank you. And you hail my fave poet, Emily Dickinson.

Thanks to my soul friends for constantly boosting me. Mmmuah. Thanks to my husband Rishi, who discouraged me from getting into too much slang :)

1. Cornucopia

A great distance it can seem

Flashes of rainbow, next to a stream

Ride and ride my dear fellow

Don't look back, keep it mellow

The sun rises every single day

Keeping all of the dark at bay

Lest you tend to give up hope

It's not really the end of the rope

Pride and prejudice serve no one

Joy and freedom are next to none

The only stars that shine bright

Are the ones that are in sight

Passion and zest are godly

Inward or outwardly

The strength shouts from within

Why o why don't we begin

That we want each day is utopia

Mastering the mind is real cornucopia.

#iwritewhatyoufeel

2. Lost and Found

LOST AND FOUND

In the veil of the sun

I saw them as one

Mighty cats I took this pic

As I leaned over the edge quick

As you moved with stealth around your mate

She purred with love, never with hate

We learn many a thing from you, O beast

To say smart survival is the least

Bred in captivity is unfair

But what do we do for better care?

In the midst of those vast meadows

I can see two three other shadows

The mystery of the forest is deep

I wander further to take the leap

Majestic cats your aura is bright

We love you whether orange or white ...

- Amritha

#creaturesofhabit #zootopia #bornfree

P.s - a visit to the zoo today

3. Hanu-"man" - we have a superman!

We also have a superman - he's Hanu"MAN".

Omnipotent Anjani putra

Bravery is you, O Veera!

Loyalty is your middle name

Never giving up on Raavan's game

It's Lord Rama that makes you strong

Shielding Maa Sita all along

As you rushed Sanjeevani to heal

Lakshman' s fatal injury was no big deal

Millions pray to you for health

Knowing it is one's only true wealth

Vayuputra you battle with wit

With deep love our hearts are lit

Turning impossible into the possible

Making us feel so much less vulnerable

You are a true warrior of the ages

O Hanuman! We bow to you, and so do sages!

#Hanuman #GoodGod #epic #loyalty #india #ramayana
#marvelmania #heroes

4. OMEN

OMEN

A "Woman" is NOT

"Woo" men, NOT

"Woe" men, NOT

"Shoo" men NOT

"Whoa!" men but they need

"Gentle" men, who are wing "men"

With a wee bit of acu "men"

And an independent regi"men'

And if that is NOT happening comrade...

Just say AMEN! ♦♦

- Akarsha

And #viceversa !

#youknowifyouknow #amor

5. KALKI

Kalki, such a proud movie. :)

"Amma vacchindhi" - is eternal. (Mother has finally come!)

We all are bouncing between birth and rebirth. The old and the new.

We are blending in more and more mythology, yay and super yay to that ⊠. Indian cinema is getting "larger than life" and leaping delightfully and crazily by staying true to its roots. 👏.

Fave - #Ashwatthama 🏹 #kaira 🪶 #shambala🏯

#kalki2898AD Three cheers to Vyjayanthi Movies, Nag ashwin garu and team ⊠⊠ ☆ ☆ ☆ ☆ . A small poem.

"The Last Emperor"

"Bhairava stands tall
Rediscovers one and all
Sumathi redefines birth
Though she sees no joy or mirth

Supreme is blinded by greed
Gambling with every mother indeed
Bujji is the transformer galore
Making digs at her master even more

Ashwatthamma, the guru, aces it all
For the future of humanity is his clarion call
He is the ancient warrior bard
Defeating new age evil and standing guard

The RISE of Kalki will be the real dawn
When is the divine being born?
The moment will be super illuminating
Where is the divine descending?"

- Amritha

#prabhasrajuuppalapati #deepikapadukone
#AmitabhBachchan and #bujji #thelastemperor #kalki

6. Pebble

#Pebble 🖤

https://www.instagram.com/p/CwFtZhToWII/

What can we learn from Pebble
To love her shell double
To be as gentle as a sage
To be steady even without a cage
To not compete with the hare
To do things you love and not dare
To stay with the greens for fuel
To avoid all meat, to not be cruel
She is one of the eternal optimists
She knows all the turns and twists
Just be like Pebble
Avoid all the rubble 🐢

P.S.- Loophoop kids makes nice crochet toys for a cause.

@loophoopkids #instamood #instagood #tortoise
#wildthings #lookcomfy #crochet #instamoment #telltale
#toystory #cheers #instalove

7. SEEDS

A teacher is not a preacher -

She gauges us ably to share

All that knowledge we need to dare

She laughs with us every single day

While we drive her crazy hey hey hey

For sure she knows each of our tricks

And we know that we really were pricks

She shapes, she molds and advises

We grumble then, but later our brain realizes

She is that parent away from home

Who talks about all -rectangles to Rome

As we wait to dash to the library

She just smiles on the contrary

Bunking classes for the sports day thrill

She is on the field with us to support our will

We know who our teachers are

Anyone who inspires, near and far

What can we then give back to our mentor

Except gratitude, come summer or winter.

-Amritha

#forgetmenot #piilars

8. Ram Setu

A bridge appeared long long ago

Some believed it was a rescue mission

Some said it was nature's vision

While people in kaliyug questioned all of it

It was divine play, speculators never got this bit

The spirit behind phenomena is always one

That the mystical does exist, second to none!

#RamSetu #monkeymind #modernmen #adamsbridge #abridged

Think.

#deepwaters

9. Oka maata (A word)

O manava!

Nee aasa loney undhi nee anubhavam,
nee baasha loney undhi oka paravasam,
nee swaasa loney undhi nee praanamu,
nee sparsa loney undhi nee baavamu,
nee drushtiloney undhi nee daivathvamu,
Nee chethiloney undhi nee jeevithamu!

- (in Telugu)
#telugu #teluguvelugu #mothertonguemorals

10. On Cloud Nine

"ON CLOUD NINE"

They say there is the silver lining
But it's hard to see it
when you are whining
They say it pays to look up
But the world chooses to interrupt
When the clouds are desolate and dark
Wait for that sun
to look at that spark, and make your mark.
Hot lemon tea
Sip oh so fresh
Sit on the deck
With nature we mesh.
Poets wrote things
with hope
Mustered their courage
in order to cope, without dope
Good tidings are often found
Depending on the things we surround.
Just look all around.
Definitely not at all at the ground.

#wordsworth #dothework #kaleidoscope
#instagood #instadaily #iwritewhatyoufeel

11. Mavericks

A hero does not wield a gun
Yet he has the ability to stun
He rises to demons all around
Some are inner ones, not easily found
The tunnel is oh so long and dark
But there is light at the end, so look for that spark
Even zero is on fire when placed right
So keep the faith and face the fight.
Laugh out loud all the way
Do the jig, but do not sway.

- Akarsha

#captainmarvel #allrise #hopeisdope

12. Mr Grumpy

There was once a cross old lad
He drove everyone quite mad
His wife pleased him a lot
But he kept asking when, why, what
She laid down that pot of tea
And wondered if he would ever be in glee

His colleagues even wondered
Why Mr Grumpy thundered
His kid thought he was unfair
That he scorned often at what she would wear

Mr Grumpy went to the library
Reading is really what was primary
The man had no friends or so he thought
Not once did folks think why he fought

Mr Grumpy had no good company
Not even to enjoy his favorite symphony
One day his wife called his friends
Told them Mr Grumpy easily offends
They decided to pop in and greet
A long time since they had a meet

The next day they all poured in
Nudged Mr Grumpy who actually flashed a grin
They talked and talked till they convulsed with joy
Every single one was a little boy.

Oh Mr Grumpy just needed to be understood
Once again as he met his childhood. :)

- - Akarsha

#oldisgold #storiesnevertold

13. What's Up

The ping from that thing
And the kind of hope it brings
It could be a pal or a gal
We were waiting for that call

As addictive as rich cake
Messages that make us shake
Either with anger or with joy
Could be a ruffian or a kind boy

Every forward every share
Could be nice or a nightmare
It is really the spam we hate
Unless it's is from a soulmate

Voice notes are a delight
Give us less scope to fight
Emojis set the tone
But the wrong ones can burn

Group chats drive us crazy
Than please all be rather lazy
Family members are rather bland
Give opinions before we can take a stand

Our friends frown at imagined favoritism
Though some bullies bring alive that realism
There is no escape from this twiddling thumb
To even think of life without it is dumb!

Say what's up responsibly
Say what is needed consciously
If everyone uses it fairly
Then life will be loved clearly!

Akarsha
PHEW!

14. Food swings

Ding dong!

There is our Zwiggyy guy
Just outside our door
And how it has changed life
It makes us want more

Baked goods to raw foods
They have them all
All we do is swipe
And have a tummy ball

I can tell you this much my friend
Diner Dash is unfortunately not a trend
This new way of life has its pitfalls
Parents screaming no more food calls

Cook at home they say
And we know they are right everyday
We know not the bad cooking oil they use
Our bellies growl and grunt with abuse

Choose health with a salad daily
Even if those tempting tacos loom largely
Do you think people will ever realize
That they just cannot choose wise

We can't have the cake and eat it too
We have to decide and think it through!

Ding dong! Oops.

- Akarsha

15. Supermodel

She sashays down the ramp
She is certainly not a tramp
Her shiny rosy lips
And her unmistakable swaying hips
Arrest one and all around
So much awe can be found

She knows her mind and matter
She is no slave to the ones who flatter
She is a brand on her own
Even without the show stopper gown worn
As her deep gaze is steady
She makes us all quite heady
To take on the world by stride
After hidden battles one can't confide.

A supermodel is the one
Who truly feels second to none
It comes from her inner light
Which shines so ever bright ..

Love. Akarsha

16. Mr and Mrs

Husbands and wives
Not always forks and knives
Need lots of love
And blessings of the one above

Tolerate and endure are definitely on the team
This comes easy if one support each others dream
Every marriage is conscious care
Every phase reveals a new dare

She complains of him not talking more
He spouts of needing some space indoor
No matter how modern today's age
They do need the true wisdom of a sage

Nurture and care my fair lady
Provide for the loved ones oh dear daddy
Or switch roles as needed
As society always pleaded

As both of them stride along independent, but together
They are bound to feel gratitude in any weather.

Love always
Akarsha

17. Mon oncle

My uncle, my buddy
Who saved me from getting muddy
Who brought many a twinkle
More precious than a blue carbuncle

I can tell he was divine intervention
Not a man of convention
His aura spreads other's wings
He even pays attention to little things

God please help uncle shine
Who never thinks in terms of mine
He is an angel on earth
He is a true man of mirth, visiting every home and
hearth.

There comes along an angel sooner or later
Just a matter of time before you turn greater ...

Akarsha.

18. Affairs

They please
They tease
One wants a life with ease

They prod
Take away God
And you think they are spared the rod

But consequence there will be
From then to eternity

Choose your fate
It's never too late.

Affairs are no fairs ...

- Akarsha

19. Black Dog

It makes you feel numb
It makes you want no crumb
It makes you feel so worn
It makes your insides torn

Most people are fighting for hope
Life seems at the end of a rope
Most people don't understand
About how it makes life bland

Pills are a desperate move
Just to find your normal groove
The roots are in our childhood
Usually not so very good

It could be a sexual scar as a child
It could be an abusive parent not so mild
It could be early death of a loved one
It could be bullying next to none

Trauma rises as we grow
It's scary to go with the flow
Neighbors judge quickly with ease
Opinions never do cease

BUT, mindfulness shows us the light
Meditation triggers insight
Service diffuses our plight
Support restores our might.

(for all brothers and sisters, depression can be dealt with
loving support, non addictive medical care and being
close to nature.)

- Akarsha

20. Green Eyes

1

He looked at her post
With a sort of dread utmost
A thousand likes from every folk
Their own love seemed like a joke

He knew she was a pure soul
And it made him feel without a goal
She was sincere when she spoke
He knew she was why he awoke

He kept watching her mission
And he had a zeal to mirror her passion
He started to self develop more
He started seeing life roar

She looked at him with so much love
He knew it was a bond from heaven above
She applauded him as he rose
He hugged her tight of course

Green eyes, you are really clear
Self work is how you beat any envy, cheers!

21. Aakasavani

A melody he composes
It's very deep, not all roses
You know when you hear the song
You want to hear it all along
His voice stirs the soul
Can feel incredibly whole
With mostly baritone and a chord
We can tell he is the lord
Raagam thalam all bold
Nothing short of gold
Dear sir, it's not about the Golden Globe pages
This adulation had been there since ages
You made India dizzyingly proud
The echo is far and loud.
Every song is trance
For mythology, mystery or romance.
It could be love or a waging war
Keeravani sir, you always set the bar.

- Akarsha

A tribute to my fave maestro MM Keeravani (MM
Kreem), an Oscar winner from India.

[url=https://www.facebook.com/photo/?
fbid=10160260878384597&set=a.418329784596&__cft__[0
]

[/url]

www.ingramcontent.com/pod-product-compliance
Lightning Source LLC
LaVergne TN
LVHW010925200726

843509LV00013B/2083